WALKING IS OVERRATED

WALKING IS OVERRATED

AN AUTOBIOGRAPHY

C E C I L   S .   P A U L

WALKING IS OVERRATED
AN AUTOBIOGRAPHY

iUniverse books may be ordered through booksellers or by contacting:

iUniverse
1663 Liberty Drive
Bloomington, IN 47403
www.iuniverse.com
1-800-Authors (1-800-288-4677)

ISBN: 978-1-5320-2319-4 (sc)
ISBN: 978-1-5320-2320-0 (e)

Library of Congress Control Number: 2017906890

Print information available on the last page.

iUniverse rev. date: 06/06/2017

ABOUT THE AUTHOR

I believe everyone has a story to tell. This is mine.

I am 81 years old. I have been married three times and have four children, two boys and two girls. I have 10 grandchildren and seven great grandchildren.

I was in the work force for 41 years, 35 with the Federal Government of Canada and six with the Hanley Corporation, the local Tim Hortons franchise in Belleville, Ontario, where I now live. I was a member of the Board of Directors of the local chapter of the MS Society for 18 years and served on the Trenton District Council of the Boy Scouts of Canada for five years. I wrote five books (not quite of the James Patterson or John Grisham level). I worked at a local speedway for 10 years where I wrote many articles for the local newspapers. I have been hit by two cars and a train and I survived them all.

My travels have taken me to Florida many times when my wife and I owned a mobile home there. I have been on two Caribbean cruises and three trips to Las Vegas. I have been to the east coast of Canada three times, once by train, once by air and once by car. I travelled from Halifax, Nova Scotia to Belleville by train alone and was treated like royalty by the staff. I took my family on a five week camping trip to Northern Ontario, and went on four trips to Michigan Speedway, located near Detroit, Michigan.

I almost forgot to tell you that I was born with no use of my legs and have been in a wheelchair all my life. I drove my own car until two unsuccessful rotator cuff surgeries ended my driving abilities.

I hope my story will inspire other people with a handicap. There is no limit to the things you can accomplish. I don't believe in feeling sorry for myself because there is always someone out there that is worse off than me. I learned at an early age that it takes all kinds of people to make up this crazy world we live in. There are short ones, fat ones, skinny ones and tall ones. They come in all shapes, colours and sizes. I'm easy to spot. I'm the one in the wheelchair.

MY EARLY YEARS — GROWING UP IN TICHBORNE

First, let me tell you about two extra-ordinary people who had a big influence on my life. They were my mother and father.

In 1839, a family of Irish immigrants under the leadership of a man called Moses Paul came from Northern Ireland and settled in Lanark County, Ontario. It was late in the year when they arrived in the area. They never had time to build a cabin before winter set in so they lived in a cave all winter. I guess that makes some of my ancestors cavemen. You can't get more Canadian than that!

A settlement sprang up in Lanark County and it was called Paul Land and was later changed to Poland, Ontario.

James Lancelot Paul was born on October 18th, 1903, the son of John Albert Paul and Agnes McDougall, owners of the general store in the tiny village of Poland. Lance's aunt asked if she could give him his middle name. She was reading a story about King Arthur at the time and thought that Sir Lancelot was a real cool guy. James grew up called by his middle name only, either *Lance* or *Lancie* but never James. His mother died when he was only four and a half years old and he was raised by his Aunt Eva.

Lance Paul was what you would call short by today's standards. He was a compact five foot, three inches tall and never weighed over 160 pounds in his life. He held many jobs in his younger years. Two of them were as a lumberjack and a wheat harvester in Western Canada. Lance finally got a steady job in 1927 which would last for the next 41 years. He was hired by Newton Garrett who was section foreman on the Canadian Pacific Railway in the village of Tichborne, Ontario.

When you tell people you are from Tichborne, the first comment you hear is "*Where in hell is Tichborne?*" I'll tell you. It's a small village with a population that never seen over one hundred. My father, who was a man of great wisdom, said that "the population never changed because whenever a baby was born, some guy had to leave town". Tichborne is on the main line of the CPR, approximately 100 miles east of Toronto by rail and eight miles south of Sharbot Lake on Highway 38 by road.

The Kingston and Pembroke Railway ran from Kingston to Renfrew and crossed the CPR main line at Tichborne. It was known as the K&P railway even though it only went as far as Renfrew and made one round trip a day, starting from Kingston. I had many a ride on the old *Kick and Push Railway* (a nickname given to the K&P railway by people of the area). The many lakes around Tichborne are famous for fishing and anglers from all across Canada and the United States come there in the summer months.

Newton Garrett moved to Tichborne from Sharbot Lake in 1918 with his family of eight daughters and three sons. He had been promoted to CPR section foreman in that year. Lance Paul was only interested in one of the Garrett girls. Her name was Lila.

Lila Pearl Garrett was born on November 10th, 1907, in Sharbot Lake, Ontario. She was 20 years old when she and Lance got married on April 20, 1927 in Lanark, Ontario. They moved to Tichborne in the same year and settled down and soon began to start a family.

John (always called Jackie) was born in 1929 and Donald came along in 1933.

The year was 1931 when tragedy struck my family. My two year old brother Jackie contracted spinal meningitis and suffered irreparable brain damage. He would have violent seizures and it would take all my parents could do to hold him down till they passed. They had to do this to keep him from hurting himself, as well as others.

My mother took him to a doctor in Kingston every week. As there was no train returning to Tichborne until the next day, it required an overnight stay in a hotel which was a big expense.

I made my grand entrance, with great difficulty, on Wednesday, September 18th, 1935. Back in the day, women had their babies at home with the aid of a mid-wife which was usually a neighbour woman. I had to be different as I was not coming out head first which was the normal way. I was going to be what is called a breach birth. I was coming out feet first and it was going to be a very difficult birth under the best of conditions.

A doctor was called in from Verona which was about 15 miles south of Tichborne. It was hoped he could turn me around and get me going in the right direction. The doctor waited out in his car until he was called in to the house. While he waited, he drank and by the time he was called on to do the delivery, my mother said he was loaded and I don't mean with medical knowledge. He was the only experienced person available. He was unable to get me turned around. When I finally was born, it was feet first. The doctor pulled me out by my legs.

What you get in this situation is an impaired doctor trying to perform a tricky medical procedure with the closest hospital in Kingston, 40 miles away. The result was a small baby boy who would never be able to walk. The muscles in both my legs were permanently damaged. My mother took me to Sick Children's Hospital in Toronto where I spent two weeks but there was nothing they could do. The damage to the leg muscles was too extensive.

I learned a long time ago to play the cards you have been dealt. I have never felt sorry for myself but have always tried to do the best with what I have. I have spent all of my life with no use of my legs and have learned to adapt to most conditions.

I was born at a time when people usually kept their children at home if they were handicapped. Not my mom and dad. As soon as I was old enough to travel, it was off to Carleton Place, Ontario, to visit my Aunt Vera and Uncle Stewart. There were no wheelchairs back then. My Dad carried me and proudly showed me off to everyone he met.

In the same year that I was born, my Grandfather (Newton Garrett) retired from the CPR and moved his family to Clyde Forks, Ontario. It was on the main line of the K&P Railroad approximately 35 miles north of Tichborne. I had many a ride on the old *Kick and Push Railway* from Tichborne to Clyde Forks to visit my grandparents during the summer. It was only 35 miles but took three hours by train. It stopped at every little village and settlement along the route.

When it was time to start school my parents found out that I had to be six years old on the day school started. Because of my birthday being on September 18th, I missed by two weeks so had to wait until the following year.

Mom borrowed books from the school and home schooled me. When the next year rolled around, the teacher had known what my mother had done and with a few simple tests, put me in grade two. Some parents were not happy but they soon got over it.

I attended a one room, one teacher school house which was approximately a mile from where we lived. My brother Don took me by wagon or bicycle in the summer and toboggan in the winter. We only missed days if we were sick which wasn't very often. My class was made up of four students. I had the same classmates for seven years. You might say we got to know each other pretty well.

The first day of school was very scary for me because I thought the other kids would call me names and make fun of me because of my handicap. My fears were short lived. A few kids did laugh at me but big brother took care of that in short order. Don was a big kid and he took no crap from anyone, especially when it concerned me.

I loved winters when Don or my friends would come and get me to go toboggan riding. I didn't like it when Doctor Mom made sure I had my daily dose of cod liver oil for cold prevention. It smelled like dead fish and tasted like thick motor oil. I never complained because it worked. If I did get a cold it was treated with Moms home made mustard plaster. It was rubbed on my chest at bedtime. It got very hot and would draw the cold out. I remember one time that she used too much mustard and burned my chest but my cold was gone in the morning. It was one of many home cures that I lived with back in the day. There was no drug store to run to if you got a cold or any other childhood medical problems. You were treated at home by the person who knew you best – your Mom. If Mom would ask me if I had a poop that day and I said no, it was castor oil time. It was like cod liver oil without the smell.

When Jackie was eight years old, my parents were faced with a decision that no parent should ever have to make. Jackie required constant supervision and his seizures were becoming more frequent. He was at the stage when he was a danger to both Don and I. He was very strong for his age and getting more violent. He would take these seizures at any time and any place. He wasn't mean. He just didn't realize what he was doing. When I was two years old and Don was four, we were very sick with pneumonia. Mom went out to the bathroom which was the outdoor type and was only gone for a few minutes. When she returned, Jackie had thrown both Don and I outside in the snow in our pyjamas and locked the door. It goes to show you how quickly things can happen and how dangerous that incident could have been.

My parents placed Jackie in the Ontario Hospital School in Orillia, Ontario, which was a facility that looked after children like Jackie. Some old biddies in the village thought it was a terrible thing to do but people who knew what mom and dad were going through, supported their decision. My mom cried for weeks but it was for the best.

Every week without fail, Dad would buy the Toronto Star Weekly Weekend Magazine and take out the coloured comic section, place two chocolate bars inside, wrap it up and mail it to Jackie. Mom would take the train to Orillia at least once a month to visit him. She was allowed to stay overnight at the facility so she could spend a couple of days with him.

A new facility opened in 1951 in Smiths Falls, Ontario and Jackie was transferred there a year later. It was a lot closer for Mom to travel.

In April 1963, Jackie got very sick and was rushed to Kingston General Hospital where he died of pneumonia on April 17th of that year. He was only 34 years old.

I remember the Second World War very clearly. During the war years from 1939 until 1945 our radio was always on during the evening news. We had several relatives serving overseas, both in Europe and in the South Pacific.

Cans were never thrown in the garbage. My brother Don and I would cut the tops off them and flatten them out. Once a month the cans were picked up by a truck from Kingston. They would be recycled into steel to build tanks and other military vehicles. In the summer school kids would collect milk weed pods and place them in large bags to be picked up and sent to Kingston as well, to be used in the manufacturing of synthetic rubber.

Food was rationed and families were issued with ration books on a monthly basis. Some of the items that were rationed were eggs, butter and meat. Dad stopped eating butter and mom would use those coupons for us boys. Until the day he died, he never ate butter again, having been so used to eating his toast on the dry side.

May 8th, 1945 started out as a regular school day until all hell broke loose around noon. A lady from down in the village, came running up the road to the schoolhouse, ringing a bell and yelling at the top of her lungs. I can still remember what she was screaming. *"The war is over!"* By the time the teacher said "class dismissed", she was talking to herself.

When the war ended in 1945, my Uncle Ormond, Dads brother, returned to Canada and came to stay with us in Tichborne for awhile. I learned about the horror of war that Uncle Ormond lived with when he served overseas for five years and was one of the lucky ones. He came home in one piece. He had many stories to tell of what went on over there during his tour of duty in the Canadian army. We would sit around and listen to him for hours. Some of his tales of battles with the enemy were very bloody and were not told to me. After all, I was only ten years old at the time.

In the late 1940's a United Church student minister by the name of Clare Kellogg came to Tichborne. He was a very special and caring person. The church was two miles from the village. Why they ever built it so far from the village, I never could figure out. Every Sunday night without fail, he would stop at our place and pick up my Mom and take her with him to attend the evening service. Dad was not a church going person. His excuse was that someone had to stay home and look after Don and I.

Clare Kellogg did a lot for the village besides preach on Sunday nights. He started a boy scout troop and cub pack in Parham, a village two miles south of Tichborne. My brother Don and I were quick to join.

Don and I in our scout and cub uniforms

LIFE BEGINS IN TRENTON
SCHOOL DAYS

This wagon was my only means of transportation when I moved to Trenton. I had to wait until someone came along to provide the power. Every spring as far back as I can remember, my Dad bought me a new wagon. The lifespan of a wagon was about a year as it got a lot of rough usage.

In 1947 Dad was promoted to CPR section foreman in Trenton, Ontario and we moved there in the summer of 1949.

Shortly after our arrival in Trenton I received a visitor. His name was Mr. Rawson from one of the local service clubs and he had a wheelchair for me. That chair changed my life. It was chain driven, made mostly of wood, was big and cumbersome, did not fold up and weighed over a 100 pounds. It was the most beautiful thing I had ever seen. No more waiting for someone to come and take me some place I wanted to go. I was independent for the first time in my life.

I could go as I pleased and I did. I put a lot of miles on that chair when I first got it.

In 1949, a local business man ran a weekly series in the local paper called *'The Man of the Week'*. The following item appeared as number 5 in the series.

Cecil Paul was born in Tichborne, Ontario, a small village north of Kingston, Ontario. Born with complete paralysis of both legs, his determination and success in the face of this handicap make him a standout among his fellow men and should serve as an inspiration to all.

Cecil didn't start school until he was seven and today at 14 is in First Form at Trenton High School. He is a great reader of current affairs and is an enthusiastic photographer. His talent in drawings cartoons is well known to his friends and family. He is a member of the local Air Cadet Squadron.

Son of Mr. and Mrs Lance Paul of 300 Sidney Street, Cecil's indomitable spirit and ever-quick smile rank him high in the esteem of his friends and fellow students.

This article appeared in the Trenton, Ontario paper in 1949

I was the first entry for the month. One person was then chosen to be Man of the Month. The 12 Men of the Month were voted on with the winner chosen as Man of the Year. A young man by the name of Jack Yarrow saved a small girl from drowning in the river. He was chosen as Man of the Month in the same month I was in. He went on to be Man of the Year. I was satisfied with my moment of glory as Man of the Week.

In the summer of 1949 Don and I came down with the worst case of chicken pox you ever saw. We spent a very uncomfortable couple of weeks in isolation in our bedroom. I still have a few scars left over from that ordeal. It was the week of our final exams that would get us into high school. I got through on my years work but Don had to write his finals and failed. He said he wanted to quit school and get a job. He was two years older than me and did not want to go to high school and be in the same grade as me. It would be very embarrassing to say the least. Dad figured that if Don had enough schooling he would put him to work and hired him as a section hand on the railroad. Don proved to be a hard worker.

That same year, we moved to a house located directly across the street from the high school. I still needed someone to take me around to the different classes. '*Wheelchair Accessibility*' was not in anyone's vocabulary back in the day and there was no elevator, even though the school was two stories high. I had no trouble getting one of the big lads to give me a piggyback from class to class. No one ever refused. The guys and gals were super. They treated me like one of their own. I made a lot of friends during my four years at good old Trenton High. I joined the air cadets and was on the student council for every year I was there.

I believe that the years spent in high school are some of the best years of your life.

I am in the front row – second from the left

This is a good comparison with my old wooden chain driven chair on the top. The light weight chrome chair on the bottom was much lighter and easier to peddle. I could go downtown to see a movie or just go for a coffee. My chair soon became a familiar sight on the streets of Trenton. As best that I can remember, I was the only person that went downtown in a wheelchair at that time. I was also in air cadets all four years I was in high school

Dad had this chair custom made just for me and it cost $250.

The chair I have now cost $10,000. I guess that's known as inflation.

One winter evening there was a high school dance just across the road from home. It was not far for me to go even with a bit of snow. I always attended the dances as I was the guy at the door taking tickets. It turned out not to be a good night as I was hit from behind by a drunk driver. I was completely airborne and ended up head first into a snow bank. I escaped with minor bruises but my chair was a write-off. The guy that hit me was my next door neighbour. I was being a nice guy, so I never phoned the police. He promised to pay to fix my chair if I didn't call the cops. Until this day I have never received a cent from him. So much for being nice and giving someone a break.

Dad replaced that chair with a regular fold up manual chair.

SPOTLIGHT STAFF

I am in the centre at the desk, just left of the teacher. Trenton High had a year book called the *Spotlight*. I was on their staff during the four years I was in high school.

ENTERING THE
WORK FORCE

I graduated from high school in 1953 and already had a job waiting for me. I became a bookkeeper for a local car dealership for a short while and then became a taxi dispatcher. It was 12 hours a day and six days a week. There was no such thing as minimum wage. My pay was as low as you could go at forty bucks a week. It was not really a dream job but I was earning my own money.

I was job hunting continuously as I couldn't see myself being a taxi dispatcher the rest of my life. It would be a terrible waste of a high school education. The taxi office was small and crowded. It was usually full of seedy characters looking to buy a bottle of whiskey. It was a well known place by the police who dropped in at least once a day. They overlooked a lot as the owner of the taxi was the son of a very prominent business man. My desk drawer was always well stocked with booze and I was told who to sell it to. I lived in fear of being caught by the police. The office smelled of cigarette smoke, sweat and whiskey. It was not a very desirable place to work in and the sooner I could get out of there, the better.

In the summer of 1954 I saw a help wanted ad in the local newspaper. It was for a clerk's position, working for the Federal Government at the

Canadian Forces Base Trenton. I filled out an application form and wrote the civil service exam, along with 25 other people. There was only one position available.

Two weeks later, after I had given up on the government position, I received a call from the civil service department at the Base. They offered me the job I had applied for. They wanted to know how soon I could start. I talked to the taxi owner's dad and told him of my job offer. He congratulated me, shook my hand and wished me luck. I called the civil service personnel clerk back and told her I could start the next day.

My first day at my new job.
The shirt and tie was to impress the boss.

On Wednesday, October 18th, 1954, I began a career that would last me for the next 35 years and five weeks. I will always remember that date. It was my Dad's birthday. I became employed as a clerk in the supply section at the Canadian Forces Base Trenton, the largest military establishment in Canada.

On a February afternoon in 1955, I was downtown Trenton in my wheelchair when I was approached by a well dressed gentleman who wanted to know if he could buy me a coffee as he wanted to talk to me. I was hesitant at first but he didn't look like a serial killer or a robber, besides I was curious as to why he wanted to talk with me. I agreed and as we headed to my favourite restaurant called the Boston Cafe.

He told me that he had seen me on several occasions but was not sure how I would take to being approached by a complete stranger. He introduced himself and told me his name was Don Rochester and he was a Colonel in the Canadian Army, stationed in Ottawa. He came to CFB Trenton on military business once in a while. He told me he was interested in why I was in a wheelchair. He said that he contracted polio when he was very young. The doctors told him that he would never be able to walk again. He was determined to prove them wrong. He continued to exercise his legs and at the age of 18, he joined the Canadian Army and soon became a physical instructor.

We talked for hours and I felt like I had known him all my life. A couple of weeks later, Don called and wanted to come and meet my parents. He came to our house and made me an offer that would be hard to refuse. He had been planning a vacation to Florida and wanted to take me with him. He said it would not cost me a cent as he would pay all the expenses.

My problem was that I only been working on the Base for only a couple of months and had no leave entitlement and I did not want to do anything to jeopardize my job. I talked to my supervisor on the Base and explained my dilemma. He granted me two weeks leave without pay and Don and I were on our way.

He and I were both history buffs so we stayed a full day in Washington D.C. to see all the monuments. While we were parked on Pennsylvania Avenue trying to get a photo of the White House, we had unexpected company. A D.C. police car pulled up behind us. They were not a bit interested in our story of wanting to get a picture of the president's house and that we were tourists from Canada. We were ordered to leave the area at once and it would be advisable not to return.

Our journey was quite an adventure. We were in all of the southern states from Virginia to Alabama. The easiest way to explain some of our exploits is to list them but not necessarily in order;

- Almost ran out of Washington D.C. by the Capital City Police for getting too close to the White House, just to get a picture.
- Stopped by State Troopers in Tennessee for speeding. The speed limit was posted as *"Safe and Reasonable"*. I guess 120 mph didn't fit into either as those categories.
- Exotic food to me was fish and chips or steak and mashed potatoes so it was great to eat in high end restaurants for two whole weeks. Don encouraged me to try different items on the menu. Some things I couldn't even pronounce. During our trip I ate turtle soup, rattlesnake soup and even ate pony steak. I asked the waitress what a pony steak was. She asked me if I knew what a pony was. I told her of course I did.
- I ate key lime pie which was delicious.
- We went into the underground caves in Kentucky. They were not wheel chair accessible but that was no problem. Don just put me on his back and away we went. I weighed less than 100 pounds at the time.
- We went deep sea fishing off the coast of Key West. It was an overcast day so I took my shirt off which was a big mistake. I was badly burned and Don had to call a doctor. Believe it or not we found one who did house calls. He came to our motel room and informed us that I had a case of heat stroke plus a bad sunburn and I was suffering from dehydration. I spent two days in bed and learned an important lesson about the Florida sun. It is extremely hot and burns unprotected skin very quickly.
- We canoed through the everglades with a guide, of course.
- We were refused service in a fancy restaurant because we were improperly dressed. We were wearing sweatshirts and jeans and hadn't shaved that morning. Don and I both have heavy beards and did look a bit scruffy. Don explained that we were from

Canada and had been on the road all morning. When they found out we were Canadians, they changed their minds and said they would wait on us but we could not sit at the back as that was for coloured people. Being a Colonel in the Canadian Army, Don was not used to this type of treatment. He promptly told the restaurant manager, who had been called earlier, that we would go someplace else to eat.

- We took a half day boat trip through the Okefenokee Swamps in Georgia. In my opinion Okefenokee is far more dangerous and primitive than the Everglades.
- We sat in the coloured section in a restaurant in Alabama because the white section was full. It was not a good idea. We were asked to leave as serious trouble might start. In the Deep South segregation was still very much prevalent. A group of locals convinced us that discretion was the better part of valour. We took the hint and left by the most direct route out of town. They sure were a touchy bunch.
- We drove over the 7 mile bridge across the Florida Keys. The overseas highway runs from Miami to Key West. The view is out of this world with the Gulf of Mexico on one side and the Atlantic Ocean on the other.

Don and I sure packed a lot of fun and memories to last a life time into those two weeks south of the border. All good things must come to an end. Don returned to his Army duties and I went back to distributing ball point pens and typing paper. We kept in touch over the years. I spent many a fun filled weekend at Don's bachelor pad in Ottawa. There was no problem getting to Ottawa as there was always someone going that way.

Don Rochester and I taken when he visited me in Belleville

In 1969 Don Rochester came to visit me for the last time. He had recently retired and moved to Chilliwack, BC, the scene of his last posting. He took time to come and see me before heading to Western Canada. He was a very quiet man who never said much about his military career. He certainly had a lot to brag about if he had been that type of a person.

With the help of my uncle, who was a mechanic, I went to Toronto and purchased my first set of wheels. It was a 1953 custom four door Ford. It was not flashy but as I found out very quickly that it was extremely fast.

It wasn't long after I got my licence that I turned into a smart-assed speed demon. I had to be the fastest car on the street. I was always trying to impress the girls. I paid the price. I received several speeding tickets and had several accidents. They were minor but still expensive. If that was today, I would have lost my driver's licence.

I settled down when I got married to Barbara Sweet of Trenton, in 1956.

Baby Lynn with proud Mom and Dad

Our first child arrived on February 2nd, 1958. Her name was Patricia Lynn but has always been called Lynn.

In 1958 I was offered a new job to become a teletype operator and work in the Communications Centre. On 28 February, 1958, I received a letter from the Commanding Officer of the air base which read in part as follows.

In view of your satisfactory service I have been pleased to recommend and have received authorization of your permanent appointment as Teletypist 1A effective 1 March 1958.......

That was on a Friday afternoon and on the following Monday I began a career that would last until I retired in 1989. I switched from issuing pens and pencils to working in a place where I could learn a trade. It was also a promotion, from a clerk to a communicator complete with a raise in pay.

This new position was in a top secret work environment. I cannot go into detail of the type of work I did. My family was not aware of the work I performed. All I can say is that I sure was glad I took typing when I was in high school.

Typing was only one of my jobs in the Communications Centre. I could also be assigned other duties such as checking messages before they were transmitted, filing messages and other duties too numerous to mention.

I worked shift work, days, evenings and the dreaded midnight shift. I learned to adjust my body to sleep in the daytime so I could stay up all night.

Left to right:
Front Row: Cpl Y. Rene de Cotret, LAC J.J. Hudon, LAC J.A. Fraser, Cpl L. Bonin, Mrs. E. Curry, Mr. C.S. Paul, Cpl N.R. Thorne, LAC J.L. Bertrand, Cpl J.H. Shultz and Cpl N. Williams.
Second Row: LAC E.G. Thompson, LAC G.W. Goodridge, Cpl T.R. Elliott, LAC D.F. Trombley, Cpl J.A. Hamilton and LAC R.A. Scott.
Third Row: LAC J.B. Duffield, LAC T.A. Buist, Cpl G.A. McIntaggart, LAC P.M. Hegarty and LAC O.D. Julien.
Fourth Row: LAC J.N. Whittingham, LAC G.H. Crotty, LAC R.D. Steeves, LAC G.A. Stewart and LAC N.E. Pickle.
Back Row: AC1 N.L. Blades, LAC C.A. Burke, LAC V.T. Pitts, LAC J.J. Poirier and LAC C.A. Fairbank.

CFB Trenton Communications Centre in 1958
That's me - front and centre

The communications centre was divided into two distinct work areas. The main section consisted of several banks of transmit and receive teletype machines for handling unclassified messages, several typing positions, service desk and supervisors area and the all important coffee room. Off to the side was what was known as the *back room* or the crypto centre. The door to this room was always locked with access limited to four civilian communicators and a military supervisor. To work in this area these four civilians had to go to CFB Clinton, Ontario, to attend a five week course to learn this elite trade.

One of the personnel working in the classified area died suddenly of a heart attack. My supervisor called me into his office and told me that he was sending me on the crypto course at CFB Clinton to replace the deceased. He told me that he was not going to tell the people in Clinton that I was in a wheelchair because they would no doubt say they could not accommodate me as the classrooms were up a flight of stairs. I got my travel documents, climbed into my trusty Ford and headed to Clinton which is located near London, Ontario. It was about a six hour drive.

When I arrived and reported to the proper office, the Sergeant in charge starred at me and asked why I was there. That was the first time I thought anyone in Clinton realized I was in a wheelchair. He was clearly upset and wanted to know why the people in Trenton had never told him to expect someone in a wheelchair and didn't know how they were going to accommodate me on the course. I told him I was fully qualified to take the course, had the proper top secret clearance and that I was very capable of performing the duties that were required. I was told in Trenton to expect this attitude and not to let them push me around.

Not making any headway, the Sergeant finally called his supervisor, who was the man in charge of the course. That's when I met Warrant Officer Daniel Truscott. He had been talking to CFB Trenton and was aware of the situation. He just hadn't told his staff yet. He took me to the Sergeant's quarters and assigned me a room. It would be my home for the next five weeks. It was up a long flight of stairs but another civilian on the course who was going to be my room mate volunteered to help me. It meant hauling my manual chair up the stairs, one step at a time. John Ducey became not only my room mate but my friend who was always there for me. He was a friendly, outgoing and cheerful individual all the way from St. Johns, Newfoundland. He was also registered for the same course as me.

Many a night, in the wee hours of the morning, John and I made that long trip up those stairs to our room.

The course classroom was up a flight of stairs. I never had any problems as there was always someone there to help. We were unable to study outside the classroom therefore we had a lot of free time in the evenings. I spent a lot of it in the Junior Ranks club as the entrance was at street level.

I aced the course with a mark of 88.8% and when I returned to Trenton I was employed in the Crypto Centre. I worked shift work, two weeks on days, one week on evenings and then one week on midnights, and one weekend a month on call. I finally achieved a trade I loved. It was a very important position that I held. Not bad for a kid from the country growing up and accomplishing all this from a wheelchair. Another raise in pay as well as I was now a Communicator Level 2.

I never could have made it in CFB Clinton without the help of Warrant Officer Dan Truscott and John Ducey.

A year after I was in Clinton, Warrant Officer's Truscott's 14 year old son Steven was charged with the rape and murder of 14 year old Lynne Harper. He was found guilty and sentenced to hang but this sentence was later changed to life in prison. I followed this case throughout the years as I had a personal interest in it. Lynne Harper's father was my boss when I worked in the supply section at CFB Trenton. I also got to know Harper's brother when we camped together at a provincial park near Trenton.

In 1997, Steven Truscott came out in the open and let everyone know where he had been living since his release from prison. He had been residing in Guelph, Ontario. I decided to try and contact him. I sent him an email explaining how his dad had helped me years ago at CFB Clinton. I also told him how I believed in his innocence. He replied and thanked me for what I said about his father and we have been in contact ever since. Although I never met him personally, I feel that I know him and realize what he has been going through all those years. When he was found not guilty after almost 50 years, I emailed him to congratulate him on his victory.

A housing project in Trenton Ont., is giving new hope and new life for the unfortunate of the area.
Cecil Paul, crippled since birth, occupies another house for the disabled. Here he helps daughter Barbara Lynn with milk. Wife Barbara is proud of their newly acquired home.

The Toronto Star used to produce a weekly news magazine called the Star Weekly. They came to our house and interviewed my wife and I to do an article about handicapped people. I was not real happy with this picture. It was supposed to be a candid shot of myself with my wife and daughter in our kitchen doing normal things. They got my daughter's name wrong to begin with. Her name is Patricia Lynn. My wife wouldn't dress up that much to go to the Royal York Hotel. They called me "crippled" which is a word I despise and asked them not to use. They never mentioned the fact that I was employed with the Federal Government for the past several years. The story made it sound like I was a welfare case.

My first new car was a 1961 Volkswagen.
My daughter Lynn and I posing for the camera on our trip up north.

The year was 1962 when I decided to buy a new car. I chose the Volkswagen Beetle or *Bug* as it was commonly called. I forgot to mention earlier that I designed my own hand controls for my first car. They were easily transferred to any car with an automatic transmission.

The Bug was not automatic so I went to the machine shop in Trenton and had them add another level for the clutch. It sounds a bit confusing but once I had a little practice, it was no problem. I took out a few clutches before I got it figured out.

The full price of this car was $1425.00. There was no such thing as sales tax so that was the total cost of my new car.

By working overtime every chance I could, I had accumulated enough vacation time, that in 1963 I had five weeks annual leave. Barb and I decided to go on a camping trip. We planned to visit an old friend in White River in Northern Ontario. Barb was four months pregnant with our second child and we decided to take a trip before the new baby arrived.

We took the back seat out of the VW and put all our camping gear and our clothes in that space. We covered everything with our sleeping bags, leaving a big area for our five year old daughter Lynn to play and sleep. The wheelchair folded up and fit in that space as well.

We were on our way to the far north on a bright sunny morning. We told everybody not to worry and we would see them in five weeks. There was no cell phones back then for us to keep in touch so we were on our own. We saw some of the most beautiful country in Canada as we drove up the Trans Canada Highway. Going through Sudbury, we decided to spend a few days just seeing the sites and then on to Sault Ste. Marie.

We made it to White River and my friend's place. We spent a week with him and his family and had a great time.

We travelled on to Nipigon where we camped along the shores of Lake Superior. We turned north to Geraldton. We took the far north route from Longlac to Hearst, a distance of 130 miles. We left Longlac with a full tank of gas as there was nothing between there and Hearst. We had to sign in before leaving and sign out when we arrived in Hearst. The signing in was necessary. The Department of Highways gave you so long to travel the distance of 130 miles. They would come to look for you if you hadn't shown up at either Longlac or Hearst, depending on what direction you were travelling. We saw a few houses along the way and also saw several moose which we had been warned about. They told us if a moose came on the road to stop your car. Do not blow your horn as the moose may charge your car. It could be fatal as a moose was a lot bigger than our little VW bug. We arrived in Hearst without any incidents. We figured we had better start going south and arrived in Timmins, the home of the famous Hollinger Gold Mine.

They were doing tours that would take you down into the mine so we donned the compulsory hard hats and got ready to go down in the elevator. Because of safety regulations we could only go down one level with the wheelchair but it was a great experience nevertheless. We spent most of the day at and around the mine and late in the afternoon we headed to Kettle Lake Provincial Park to set up camp.

We were very pleased with our campsite, overlooking the lake, complete with a beautiful sandy beach. We met a family from Timmins who were camping across from us. We became immediate friends with them and spent several fun days there.

One sunny afternoon, everything was going great, Barb and Lynn were down swimming and I was lying back getting a tan and enjoying the rays. All of a sudden, the air got very still and the sky turned black with the clouds starting to roll. Someone was yelling to get off the beach and take cover as quickly as possible. No questions asked as Barb grabbed Lynn and headed for our tent. I never figured out why we didn't run to the car instead of a flimsy little tent.

The wind came up as we pulled down the flap and grabbed the centre pole with both our hands. We could hear the rain as it smashed into the tent and it sounded like rocks were being pelted at the canvas.

There was at least six inches of water on the floor of the tent. Lynn was sitting on our suitcase as it floated about. She was crying for her Grandma. I tried to keep a brave face, telling her it would be over soon. It was a terrifying experience for all of us. Despite the wind that threatened to tear that pole from our grasp, we hung on.

It was over as quickly as it started. I took a sneak peek out the door of our soaking wet tent and what I saw was amazing. The sun was shinning and there wasn't a cloud in the sky. The ground was white, covered with golf-ball sized hail stones and tree branches were everywhere. Our little tourist tent with the centre pole was still standing while larger tents were ripped to shreds. The sand beach was completely gone with nothing but mud in its place. I had a new appreciation of Mother Nature and how nasty she could get in such a short time.

The devastation was unbelievable with cars covered with big dents from the hail. Tree branches had smashed on top of cars and large tents completely destroyed. We survived with no harm done. Those VW's were made out of good German steel, not even a little dent.

After enjoying a week of northern hospitality we decided to head south as it was time to return to reality and back to work. Our trip home was uneventful and we arrived home safe and sound back in Trenton. We came home with some great memories of our trip to Ontario's north country. Barb, Lynn and I spent a lot of weekends camping with our little 6 x 6 tourist tent, travelling to different camp sites, mostly in Provincial Parks.

Working shift work had its advantages as I would sometimes get four days off at a time. One weekend, we went to Driftwood Provincial Park, north of Pembroke on the Ottawa River. It was a 200 mile drive but we had a lot of fun and met several new people which is what it is all about.

It rained all night on our last day and we packed up in the wet and headed home.

We were all tired and wet and only 30 miles from home when a skunk decided to cross the road in front of me. As everybody knows, a skunk never hurries and this little two-toned kitty didn't make it. I hit it dead centre. It went up over the sloped hood and onto the windshield. I tried to get it off with the wipers but it only smeared it around and made it worse. Lynn was crying, Barb was yelling and I was gagging.

It was late when we finally made it home. The first thing next morning I went to the store and bought two large cans of tomato juice. I was told it was the best thing to get rid of the odour.

Even with the car washed in the juice, soap and lots of water, it still took several days to get rid of the smell and the remains of the unfortunate jaywalker. Needless to say, my neighbours were not very happy with us but I didn't see anyone rushing to help me.

On December 23, 1963, we received an early Christmas present.
Barb gave birth to our second child. His name is Steven Donald John.
In the summer, his mother put him out on the grass to play
and he was not impressed as you can see.

708 COMMUNICATION SQUADRON TRENTON

A LOOK INTO THE PAST

Some members of RCAF Station Trenton message centre in the early 1960's: Front row, left to right - FS Kahle, S/L Bradley (BTelO), Mr. Paul, F/L Derkson and Sgt Dossett. Centre row, left to right - Sgt Johnston, Cpl St Amour, LAC Lamoureux, LAC Denham, LAC Sheppard and Cpl Walker. Back row, left to right - LAC Arksey, LAC Ash, LAC Burt, LAC Lavallee, LAC Swan, LAC Howard and LAC Vogel.

Picture taken in 1964. It was the year 708 Communication Squadron
was officially formed.

COIN COLLECTING AND WRITING – WINNING HOBBIES

Photo taken from a local newspaper in October, 1964.

I became interested in coin collecting in 1962 and joined the local club which met in Belleville once a month. The *Bay of Quinte Numismatic Association* was made up of several experienced collectors. The meetings were very helpful to me, an amateur collector. Some people collected by date, some specialized in certain denominations such as nickels only and others collected coins with errors. I was interested in collecting by type. For example, Queen Victoria had two different obverse designs. That is the front of the coin showing the Queen's head. I had all the denominations of all the Monarchs from Queen Victoria to Queen Elizabeth II. My collection showed only coins when they changed in their design. By collecting this way, I avoided the expensive coins. I soon became well known in the coin collecting circle.

The following pages are some newspaper articles that appeared in the local newspapers in Trenton and Belleville.

Cecil Paul Has Best Display in Coin Show

BELLEVILLE – The Bay of Quinte Numismatic Association's third annual Coin Show, which was held in Belleville on Saturday, was described as a huge success. There were many excellent competitive displays, several coin dealers and a large auction of several choice coins held at 3 p.m.

Out of town collectors and guests came from the United States, Toronto, Kingston, Frankford, Campbellford, Picton, Oakville and Hamilton.

The competitive coin displays were judged by three men experienced in this field. They were David Ashe of Oakville, John Regitko of Toronto and John Hodgson of Belleville.

The winners of first place trophies were: Canadian coinage, Cecil Paul of Trenton; Foreign coinage, Frank Sorenson of Toronto; Paper money, Ken Hart of Oakville; Miscellaneous, Andy Anderson of Trenton.

A trophy was also presented to Hugh Bondy and Jerry Jenkinson of Belleville for their display of medals and armed forces insignia, which decorated the whole front wall of the Kiwanis Centre.

The award for the best display in the show went to Cecil Paul, for his display of Canadian Commemorative coins.

This was Mr. Paul's 10th award for his coin displays that he has received in the last two years. These awards are not given for the value of the displays but for neatness, eye appeal and originality.

Trenton coin collector has won several prizes

Cecil Paul, 3 Ramsay Street, has competed in five numismatic shows in the past year and a half and has won first prize four times and has received one third prize.

Mr. Paul has been collecting coins for three and a half years. He is a member of the Bay of Quinte Numismatic Association, The Ontario and Canadian Numismatic Associations.

Last week he added another win to his prize list, placing first in the Dominion of Canada coin display. The display contains coins of Canadian mintage and date from 1870 to the present.

Judging of the coins is based on the 100 point system. The main body of points is given for originality, eye appeal, neatness and information on the coins displayed. Only five points is given for the value of the coins.

This weekend Mr. Paul will be competing in the largest competition in Ontario, to be held at the Royal Hotel in Toronto from October 29 to 31.

In all coin competitions little emphasis is placed on the actual value of the coin. Therefore, a person with a $50 collection stands a chance to win just as well as a person owning a $5,000 collection.

Trenton Man Wins Award in
Numismatic Exhibition

Cecil Paul, 3 Ramsay St., a member of the Bay of Quinte Numismatic Association of Belleville, and Allen Guay, also of Trenton, attended the annual Metropolitan Numismatic Club showing at the Union Station in Toronto, on April 11th. The Metropolitan is the largest coin club in Ontario and the coin show is one of the largest held for collectors.

Mr Paul took first prize for his type set collection of King George VI and Queen Elizabeth II. The first prize was a gold cup. Allen Guay of Trenton, won third place in the competitive displays with his display of Dominion of Canada 5 cent collection.

These displays have little bearing on value and are judged on originality, eye appeal, and the information conveyed to the non-collecting public.

On Friday, April 17th, Mr. Paul and Mr, Guay attended the Ontario Numismatic Association second annual convention held in Ottawa at the Chateau Laurier. Guest speaker at the convention was the Master of the mint in Ottawa.

Coin clubs from all over Ontario met and competed with their coin displays. Allen Guay of Trenton took second place and Cecil Paul took third place in Canadian coins. Donald Desaulniers of Belleville also took a second place ribbon displaying Canadian coins.

The Bay of Quinte Numismatic Association met once a month at the Kiwanis Centre in Belleville. It is only a 20 minute drive east of Trenton. I never missed a meeting regardless of the weather.

One winters night the temperature was -20 when I left home in Trenton and my trusty VW got me there with no problem. It was a cold ride. There was more heat coming out of a toaster oven than there was in my Volkswagen. By the time the meeting was over and I was heading home, the temperature had dropped to -28 and falling. I was going through Bayside, a small village just east of Trenton, when I ran out of gas. I reached down to flip the little lever that would give me an extra gallon. It would be enough to get me home. The lever snapped off and I was stranded on the side of the road. I was there for over an hour in the freezing cold. A Good Samaritan finally stopped. He had a pair of vice grips to turn the broken lever and after letting the car warm up and getting the ice off the windows, I was on my way.

I came very close to freezing to death. It was a scary situation. I had no way of calling anyone as cell phones had not been invented yet.

A Sunday night tradition – our families always got together at Mom and Dad's for dinner on Sunday night.

My family is on the left: My daughter Lynn, her Mother and me. Mom is in the middle at the back. My brother Don's family is on the right. Kevin, Diane, their Mother Kay and Rodney. Dad is on the right as well. Don is not in the picture as he was the man with the camera.

This photo was taken in 1963.

**This is the latest increase to our family.
Wayne Cecil James
was born on November 13, 1969.**

I have always been interested in writing, especially stories that are of a historical nature. When I was still living in Tichborne, I drew a map of the village with every house shown by a little square with the people's names that lived there. It was for a school project. The teacher was very impressed. She even hung it up on the bulletin board at the back of the school.

I got a Smith-Corona portable typewriter for Christmas when I was in my first year in high school. It was a real surprise. It sharpened up my skills in typing and it sure came in handy when I started writing stories. I wrote a 30 page history of Trenton for the local newspaper called the Trenton Courier Advocate. It was for a special edition celebrating the 100th anniversary of the town. They printed it okay but unfortunately, not to my expectations. They broke it into numerous short stories spread throughout the paper. They only gave me credit for a small article on the front page. I was very disappointed and a bit embarrassed. My history teacher had come to our place on several occasions to proofread the story and check for errors. All my classmates were looking forward to reading it and when it came out in the way the paper did it, I was not very happy.

I am going to list some of my writing achievements but not necessarily in order.

- Wrote a book on the grading of Canadian coins.
- Wrote newspaper articles for Riverview Speedway for three years.
- Wrote a yearbook for Riverview Speedway.
- Wrote newspaper articles, weekly racing program plus kept records of races for Brighton Speedway for 12 years.
- Was the Public Relations officer for Trenton Boy Scouts for five years. Wrote many articles for local newspaper and organized special events for the local scout movement.
- Wrote a book on the murder of my Great Grandfather from Sharbot Lake, Ontario. Made several trips to the Sharbot Lake area doing research. My mother told me the story so I decided to write a book. I sold copies mostly to relatives and people from the Sharbot Lake area.
- In 1986, I wrote a weekly column on stamp collecting for an American based newspaper. My column was called *The Northern Neighbour*. My articles were always about Canadian Stamp Collecting – the only Canadian writer for the paper.
- When my step daughter was diagnosed with MS in 1996, I joined the Hastings County Chapter of the MS Society. I was on the Board of Directors for 16 years. I wrote many articles for local newspapers plus a newsletter four times a year.
- Wrote a book on Canadian stamps. It was called *From Sea to Sea* and was the history of Canada told with postage stamps. It was very popular with collectors of Canadian stamps.
- Wrote a weekly column in *The Contact,* the CFB Trenton Base newspaper. 708 Communications Squadron was known as Thumper Squadron after the Walt Disney character from the movie Bambi. *Thumper Says* was the name I gave the column.

- **NOTE: Walt Disney Productions contacted the Commanding Officer of the Squadron and told him that they could no longer use Thumper on the Squadron crest. The image of Thumper was a possible copyright infringement and could not be used on any Squadron items. Thumper was changed to an ordinary rabbit but was still called Thumper Squadron.**
- Wrote a serialized story entitled *"Paddy" Burke – Pioneer Aviator* which appeared in several instalments in *Contact*, the CFB Trenton newspaper.
- I was also Assistant Editor of this paper for several years.
- Compiled a 21 volume history of the Squadron, containing over 2000 pictures complete with captions. I worked as Public Relations Officer for the last two years prior to my retirement in 1989.
- Organized the 25th Anniversary of 708 Communications in 1989. There was no such thing as e-mail back then. Wrote letters to former members, using snail mail. I arranged hotel accommodations for out-of-towners.
- Wrote a book on the 25 year history of 708 Communications Squadron Trenton.

In 1970 our marriage fell apart and Barb moved out taking our youngest son Wayne with her. I was left to raise our oldest two, Steven and Lynn, by myself.

I had my shift changed at work. My supervisor realized the problems I was having at home. He made up a shift just for me and it was called the booster shift. It was from noon till 8 pm, the busiest time of the day in the communications centre. The hours worked out fine for me as I was able to be at home to make sure Steve and Lynn got off to school and was home not too late in the evening. Lynn was 12 years old and very capable of looking after Steve. She always had supper ready for me. I never ate so much Kraft dinner and beans and wieners in my life.

A month after Barb left, I was told that she was going to send Wayne off to Europe with her military family friends who had recently been posted to Germany. No way in hell was I going to let that happen. I contacted her to let her know she couldn't do this without my permission which she would never get. I told her I wanted Wayne to come live with me. She was happy to let him go and never tried to see him or Steve and Lynn again and our divorce was uncontested. I was a free man with three kids to raise on my own. I was not exactly good dating material.

We always went to Mom and Dads for dinner on the weekends and Mom would come over during the week if I wanted to go out.

I started to date a girl by the name of Heather who lived in Montreal and she wanted Wayne to go live with her until she could get moved to the Trenton area. She had three boys and a girl and she said that one more would not be a problem. It would also give Wayne somebody to play with during the day.

JOINING THE BOY SCOUT MOVEMENT

Wayne moved to Montreal but it was for a short time only as my lady friend left Quebec and moved in with her sister who lived in Consecon, a village approximately ten miles south of Trenton.

Needless to say I spent a lot of time in Consecon, especially on the weekends. I became interested in the Scout movement, particularly in the Presqu'ile District. The following articles appeared in the Trenton paper.

Attend Camp
By
Cecil S. Paul

The first Consecon Cubs finished the year with a camp held at the Consecon Tent and Trailer park during the first week of July. They were under the supervision of Daniel Morrissey, Cubmaster and Cecil Paul, assistant Cubmaster. Extra assistance was supplied by two activity leaders, Shawn Bloomfield of Consecon and Len Collyer of CFB Trenton who was a fellow co-worker of Cecil Paul.

The camp was officially opened and inspected by William Turncliffe, Assistant District Commissioner on Saturday afternoon.

The cubs, nine in all, worked on several badges and stars during the camp and enjoyed a trip to the fish hatchery at Codrington.

All cubs who attended camp earned four badges and their green star. The badges they received were Angler, First Aid, Woodsman and Personal Fitness. Three of the boys, John Gallant, Wayne Morrissey and Leslie Bush also received Swimming badges.

A special camp fire was held on Friday night where the presentations were made. Daniel Morrissey turned the cub pack over to Cecil Paul, who will be the new Cubmaster and Leonard Collyer, the assistant Cubmaster. Mr. Morrissey has sold his home in Consecon and will be moving to Nova Scotia in a few weeks.

Special awards were given to the following: Mr. Morrissey, a farewell gift from the boys in appreciation for the three years that he spent with the cubs in Consecon; Leslie Bush, best all around Cub; David Boudreau and David Brown, most obedient Cubs; John Gallant, best athlete and David Boudreau, best fisherman.

CUB LEADERS

The leaders of the First Consecon Cubs are left to right, Leonard Collyer, Assistant Cubmaster, Cecil Paul, Cubmaster, Gerald Collette, Assistant District Commissioner, Presqu'ile District, Daniel Morrissey, Cubmaster for three years and Shawn Bloomfield, activity leader.

Heather's oldest son John was born completely deaf and required a lot of special attention from his mother.

Heather and I realized it was time for some serious talks regarding our future. We were slowly drifting apart in our social life and the ramifications of raising seven children needed to be thought out completely. We split up permanently and I took Wayne home to live with me.

I gave up scouting in Consecon as well. I transferred my energy and the leadership skills I had learned in Consecon to the Trenton District of the Boy Scouts of Canada.

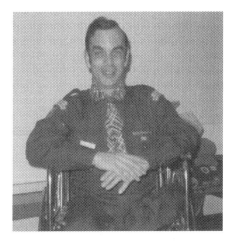

I spent a lot of time in this uniform over the next couple of years. I held two important positions with the Trenton District Council of the Boy Scouts of Canada. I was Assistant Cubmaster as well as Public Relations Officer. Both of these positions required me to attend many meetings each month and write several articles for the local newspapers, mostly on fundraising plans and events.

TRENTON DISTRICT COUNCIL SERVICE TEAM FOR 1973

Left to right: George Stewart, Assistant District Scoutmaster, Clarence Whitman, District Commissioner, Kenneth MacKay, District Cubmaster, Charles Coops, Assistant District Commissioner in charge of training, Kenneth Sears, District Scoutmaster, Front and Centre, Cecil Paul, Assistant District Cubmaster and Public Relations Officer.

During my involvement in scouting in the Trenton District I became very good friends with Ken MacKay. I spent a lot of time at meetings at his place, getting to know his family and through his wife Nancy, I met her sister Vickie.

We started dating and things got very serious in a short time. Our age difference bothered a lot of family members, including my oldest daughter Lynn. I was 18 years older than Vickie but it didn't bother us at the time but it would later on.

My family in 1973.

Lynn was 15 and just starting high school, I was next, Steven on the right. He was 10 and Wayne in the front was five years old.

I think Lynn was threatened by someone who would be taking over as head of our household.

She had been looking after the two boys for sometime and didn't need an outsider coming in to take her place.

Vickie and I decided to get married at Holloway Street United Church in Belleville for a particular reason. The pastor was Reverend

Clare Kellogg. He was my Cubmaster from Tichborne and the young man who used to pick my Mom up and drive her to church.

**Our wedding day
September 27, 1973.
Left to right: Dad, Mom, Vickie and I with her Mom on the right.**

The wedding ceremony was perfect and we all went back to Ken and Nancy's home for our reception. I only had one beer because we had to drive to Watertown in New York State, which was our honeymoon destination.

It had rained all day and most of the evening and the roads were very slippery. I turned onto Wallbridge Loyalist Road heading for the 401. This area has changed since that night. Before you reached the CNR tracks, you came to a 'T' intersection and a stop sign. You turned left then right before crossing the tracks. Vickie and I were talking and laughing and I got careless and the next thing I remember was going past the stop sign, through the ditch and smashing into the rails of the railway tracks. When we hit the rails, I flew forward into the windshield with my head and my face hit the steering wheel. My immediate concern was to check Vickie and see if she was alright. She told me she was okay but needed a minute to collect her thoughts.

I looked out to the right and saw a big yellow light that was getting bigger and bigger. I realized it was a train coming fast and knew it would never stop before it hit us.

I told Vickie to get out and run away from the car. I figured that I would get out and crawl through the ditch if I had to. When the car hit the tracks, it buckled the frame, jamming the front doors shut. All I succeeded in doing was making my head bleed more. If you have ever had a head wound you know what I am talking about. I told Vickie to climb into the back seat and pray to God the back door would open. I am glad now that I bought a four door vehicle or we would have both been killed. Vickie got out okay and at the same time two young men had been driving by and saw our predicament. They ran to the car and one guy got my wheelchair out of the trunk as the train bore down on us. The other man hauled me out over the front seat, out the back door and into my wheelchair. I knew I wasn't going to die after all.

As we were going through the ditch, I looked back just as the train hit my 1966 Acadian with the new seat covers that I put on that afternoon. The impact took the whole front off the car. It was only a matter of minutes before the crowd started to gather. Some wanted to help while others wanted to see if there were any dead bodies they could look at. A Good Samaritan had got a blanket out of his car for Vickie to lay on while she was waiting for an ambulance. The OPP and the ambulance arrived at the same time. The cop (Constable Shane Halverson) asked me what happened and I told him that I must have got careless – that remark would come back to bite my ass later on. He wanted to see my driver's license. I had a key chain with a little pouch where I kept my insurance card and driver's license. I told him if he found my car, he would have my driver's license.

With sirens blaring and lights flashing, we were off to Belleville General Hospital. They rushed us into the emergency ward where we were immediately looked at. I required several stitches in my forehead and after a nurse picked the glass fragments from Vickie's eye glasses, out of her face she told my wife she didn't need any stitches so we were good to go. The honeymoon was officially over.

As we were getting ready to leave, The OPP constable who had been at the accident scene was waiting for me. He gave me my driver's license which he had found, congratulated us on our marriage and gave me a ticket, charging me with careless driving.

I called a friend who came and picked us up. After stopping at his place for a good stiff drink, he drove us home. It was after midnight so I was surprised that Lynn and Steven were still up. Bad news travels fast. Some lame brain had phoned the house and told Lynn that we had been hit by a train and they didn't know how bad we were hurt. What a hell of a thing to tell a 15 year old kid who had been in bed sleeping. Naturally Lynn phoned Mom and Dad and they did not know anything either. A quick call to my parents to assure them we were okay, and a big hug to each of my kids, we both took our aching bodies and crawled into bed. I know I never slept much as I lay there realizing how close we had come to being killed. I guess the good Lord wasn't ready for either one of us just yet.

The following article appeared in the local paper the next day.
Area Couple Saved As Train Hits Car

Two Trenton residents are very thankful to be alive today and due to quick action received by three Belleville men, Mr. and Mrs. Cecil Paul, 4 Johnson Road, were pulled from their 1966 model car only minutes before a westbound CNR freight train hit and demolished the vehicle.

The accident occurred at 10:15 p.m., Thursday, September 27 on County Road 5a, better known as the Walbridge-Loyalist Road. The northbound driver entered the intersection at County Road 2 and continued to the north ditch and came to rest on the main line of the CNR tracks.

Mr. Paul, a paraplegic and his bride of five hours were trapped in the vehicle unable to open the doors which had been jammed in the mishap. Three passing motorists, Haigh Chalmers, 27 Applewood Drive, Patrick Haley, 12 Glen Road, and Robert Murray, 189 Pine

St., all of Belleville, managed to open the jammed doors and get the occupants out minutes before the train completely demolished the vehicle. The men did not witness the accident.

Mr. and Mrs. Paul were taken to Belleville General Hospital where they were treated for cuts and later released.

Constable W.S. Halverson of the Belleville Detachment, Ontario Provincial Police is investigating. Traffic was tied up for several hours.,

I received a court date to face the careless driving charge and had two weeks to prepare my defence. I decided to defend myself. The worse thing that could happen was a $125 dollar fine or a week in jail. The stories that I heard were pretty scary. The judge was very strict and I knew that if I was found guilty I would chose the fine as the jail was not wheel chair accessible.

I belonged to a stamp club on the Base and one of the members was in the military police. He loaned me a book showing the rules for road signs in the Province of Ontario. I made a lot of notes and found several discrepancies on the sign markings on Walbridge-Loyalist Road.

My day in court finally arrived. I told no one as I wanted to do this on my own and if I lost I didn't need a lot of family members telling me what I should have done. If I won, I would let everybody know how smart I was to defend myself.

I arrived at the court house and was sitting in the back waiting for my case to be called. I watched as the judge banged his gavel and sentenced a young man to the slammer for a week. My name was called next and I wheeled up to the front. I wish you could have seen the look on the judge's face as he asked me if I was Cecil Paul. He asked me where my lawyer was. I asked him if I could defend myself and he said I could. He told me to listen to what the constable had to say and not interrupt him. He told me I would have my chance to cross exam the constable after he had completed his testimony.

Constable Halverson began by saying when he arrived the accident was already over and my wife and I were sitting on the side of the road waiting for the ambulance. He then told the judge that he could smell beer on my breath. The judge told the clerk to strike that remark from the record as I had not been charged with drinking. That cop must have had one hell of a sniffer to be able to smell my breath from the distance that he had been from me. He then told the judge that I had been speeding because he had measured the skid marks on the pavement as I crossed the intersection. He also told the judge that he had asked me what had happened as he had not seen the accident. He stated that I told him I must have been careless so that was why he had laid that particular charge. When he was finished, it was my turn to play Perry Mason.

The judge told me that I could question the constable and also tell my side of the story. This was going to be fun. I told the judge that it had rained most of the evening and the pavement was wet. It was impossible to measure any skid marks on this type of surface and furthermore, I had never hit the brakes as I crossed the road and hit the ditch.

I then explained what was wrong with the road signs. I had my military police friend's book in front of me as I began to tell him what was wrong with the road markings. The judge asked to see the book and said I was not supposed to have it. It was only available for police officers. He wanted to know where I got it. I told him that I would rather not say. The clerk gave it back to me as the Prosecutor began to shuffle his feet a bit. I had done my homework and now it was my turn to make the constable sweat. On a rural road the stop sign must be illuminated and it wasn't. At a 'T' intersection on a rural road, the checker board sign must be at least four feet square and at a height that it was in direct line with an approaching vehicle. The one on the intersection that I went through was one foot square and nailed to a pole and was 20 feet from the ground. I had made sure because I had a friend measure it for me. It was agreed by both parties that Halverson had not witnessed the accident so how could he say I was speeding. I was finished with my defence. It was only a matter of a couple of minutes when the judge banged his gavel and said *not guilty* and dropped all charges.

I go to the Quinte Mall in Belleville quite often and have on more that one occasion ran into Shane Halverson, who is now retired. We still talk about that night long ago when we met at the scene of my car accident and our day in court. I have also met and talked to Robert Murray, one of the men who pulled me out of my car that same night. I learned that Constable Halverson passed away in 2016.

I spent several years involved in scouting activities with the Trenton District Council. I attended several training courses at Blue Springs Scout Reserve, near Acton, Ontario. I also attended and took part in a training course held at Vanderwater Park which is located on Highway 37 north of Belleville.

I wrote hundreds of articles for local newspapers. My column on scouting in the Trenton paper was a weekly item and if something special was going on there would be more.

The following are some of the newspaper stories that concern me and my involvement in scouting in the Trenton area.

Appointment Confirmed

Cecil Paul, left, long time participant in the Scout movement is seen formally receiving his Warrant of Appointment as a Scouter and as Chairman of Publicity for the Trenton District Scout Council at the annual meeting and banquet Monday night.

Making the presentation is Reverend Frank Hobbs.

RECEIVES WOGGLE

Clarence Whitman, District Commissioner, Trenton District Council of Scouting, presented Cecil Paul with his woggle after he completed Part I of his wood badge.

Cubs Hold Investiture

The 3rd Trenton Cub Pack had a little special going for them during their Wednesday night meeting which is held in Grace United Church.

After their opening Grand Howl, Cubmaster Charles Young of Trenton invested two new boys to bring his pack up to a total of 25, one of the largest and oldest cub packs in the Trenton District. The two new chums who were invested were Andrew Lisk and Dean Pokotylo, both of Trenton.

Two members of the District Service Team were on hand during the meeting. Kenneth MacKay, the District Cubmaster was accompanied by two new cub leaders of the 18th Belleville Pack, Robert Shaw, and his assistant, Carol Thorburn. These two visitors came to get some ideas for their own pack in Belleville.

Cecil Paul, the Assistant District Cubmaster was at the meeting to receive his Gilwell Woggle and Training certificate for completing his Part I Wood Badge training. He completed this course last November and has taken part in a similar training session held in Stirling, a couple of weeks ago.

It was difficult to tell who was the most proud, Cecil Paul or his son Steven, a member of the 3rd Trenton pack. Steven presented the certificate to his father and placed the woggle on his neckerchief.

Preparations Complete
For 21-Mile Scout-a-thon

TRENTON – Parents need not fear the loss of their children on roads west of here next Saturday when Scout-a-Thon 74 walkers trek 21 miles to raise funds for scouting activities in Trenton.

Walkers, expecting to be mostly scouts falling under the banner of the Trenton District Council, will be under the watchful eyes of a host of volunteer organizations.

About 300 walkers are expected to take part in the day-long event.

Preparations for the walk, the first in five years, are almost complete. Playing a big part in the council's operation is the Trent Valley Five Watters Radio Association, a group of about 25 ham radio operators.

Scouting Ahead

Weary walkers will only be picked up by clearly marked official Scout-a-Thon cars. Organizers say they hope this practice will discourage parents from picking up children between checkpoints.

Any other problems that may come up will be handled by provincial police or St. Johns Ambulance, both who will be on standby duty.

Scouts Appeal for Sponsors

TRENTON – Scout program co-ordinators here are pushing to increase the sponsorship of walkers in Scout-a-Thon '74, a drive aimed at what the Trenton District Council terms a "desperate need of funds".

This year, an additional $500 went to improvements in a camp for scouts, located on Steenburg Lake, north of Trenton.

"At present", says Scout-a-Thon co-ordinator Cecil Paul, "coffers of the council are nearly empty. A photo copying machine, needed for reproduction of leadership training material, cannot be used since funds are not available to buy paper".

"Such problems would end if the walk-a-thon, scheduled for Saturday, Sept 21, is successful", said Mr. Paul.

The push for sponsors for walkers was stepped up Thursday night during a meeting to which all service clubs in Trenton were invited.

Only three club representatives – the Rotary, the Knights of Columbus and the Oddfellows attended.

The appeal for aid was met favourably and organizers said they expect new sponsors will be found among the many members of the service clubs.

Turnout for Scout-a-Thon poor

TRENTON – Saturday's scout walk-a-thon was not the hoped for success organizers had expected as only one third of Trenton District Council members turned out to walk the 21-mile route, Cecil Paul, walk co-ordinator said on Sunday.

The council, governing a scout membership estimated at between 300 and 350, saw only 98 people trudge highways west of Trenton in an effort to raise money for town scouting activities.

"It was a poor show on the part of scouts," said Mr. Paul. "Some groups (Trenton is divided into 10) were not even represented.

"It wasn't that they didn't know it was this Saturday either. It was all laid out to them in June."

Mr. Paul was also upset at town council. "We didn't get any support from the town. Neither the mayor nor any of his representatives came out all day. There was no visible support," he said.

Support from town merchants, who donated nearly anything that scouts asked for, was good, he said. Assistance from various other groups – the Brighton OPP, the Trenton Seniors Citizens Club, and the Trent Valley Five Watters Radio Association – was top notch.

The Public Relations Officer completed the 21-mile course in his wheelchair which he is permanently confined to. Bruce Bean, a Quinte Easy Rollers member, who joined Mr. Paul in a wheelchair Saturday, did not finish the scout-a-thon – completing 12 miles before his wrists gave out.

Only 68 of the 98 starters walked the full route in Saturday's cold and wet weather. It is not know yet who completed the walk-a-thon first.

Mr. Paul, who had hoped to raise a $100 a mile sponsorship, managed $972.51 – or $46.31 a mile.

Trent Valley Five Watters president Ben Long, Jr., said 13 club members will be monitoring walkers next Saturday. The monitoring will be extensive. So extensive, that organizers will know where each child is along the route, at all times.

The finish line was at Trenton Community Gardens. Thirteen check points will be spread along the route. Eight consecutive stations will be each manned by a checker and a radio operator who will report to the Gardens the number carried by each walker.

As a walker passes a checkpoint, his or her number will be plotted on a large board. At a glance, a walker's progress can be seen.

Two radio equipped cars will patrol the route in case a youngster develops a problem between stations.

Mr. Long said Thursday this once happened: "and we had to go out and look for lost child who wasn't lost".

Final receipts from all walkers will not be known for several days, he said.

In recalling Scout-a-Thon '74, Mr. Paul had special thanks for Brighton OPP Constable Gus Riddell who escorted him along Highway from Brighton to the town limits of Trenton. Trenton police followed Mr. Paul back into town.

Without the officer's escort, he would have had to give up his efforts to compete the full 21 miles. Travel along the highway in a wheelchair would have been unsafe, he said.

Sore and tired, but pleased with his own endurance, Mr. Paul said Sunday he estimated his time at 2 ½ miles an hour, but said he was clocked by the OPP at 16 miles an hour going down the CPR overpass hill on Highway 2, west of Trenton.

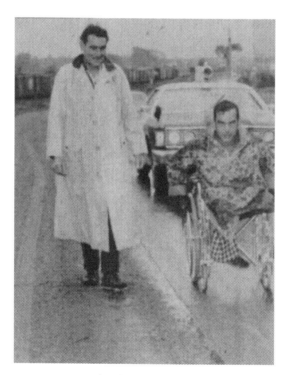

Wheeling to Victory

Cecil Paul successfully completed the 21 mile course for the Scout-a-Thon on Saturday, He was escorted by Constable Wayne Riddell in the cruiser.

Clarence Whitman, District Commissioner of the Trenton District Council, walked the entire 21 mile route with Cecil. Not at any time did Clarence push the wheelchair, although at times it would have been welcome by Cecil.

OPERATION NORDJAMB
– 75

TRENTON – Tomorrow's citizens are on our streets today. They're in our schools, they're hanging out at the corner – or at home doing chores and helping their parents and other older people who are unable to do their own chores.

A few are stealing hubcaps or cars – maybe sticking up a grocery store or gas station to get money for drugs. They're right down your street. What kind of citizens will they be? That depends on a number of things.

On whether they are with the gang on the corner – or at home helping out or whether they are dragging down the highway in a stolen car or their own souped up hot rod endangering the lives of innocent people.. They may be taking a short course in shop lifting or they may be learning first aid or camp crafts with the local scout troop.

What kind of citizens will they grow up to be? It all depends on them and on you.

You may ask yourself what you can do about it. You can make sure that boys in your community are pointed down the road to good citizenship by joining any one of the five groups in the Boy Scouts of Canada and they are all available in the town of Trenton.

Your support of local scouting makes this possible. It gives the boys in Trenton a chance to go camping – to have fun in a healthy environment – to learn what good character means through the example of some of the best men and women in your town.

Whether it is Beavers – Cubs – Scouts – Ventures or Rovers, they are all backed up by concerned and dedicated adult leaders who volunteer their time with their only reward being the satisfaction of helping YOUR boy to become a better citizen for tomorrow.

Compare this with the delinquent gangs – or the kids on the corner learning tricks from the local pusher – or aimless hostile punks just looking for trouble. What do you want in the town of Trenton? The choice is yours.

The young people of the town of Trenton are lucky in that they have a handful of these dedicated adults who spend many days of the week in teaching YOUR boys the right things and helping them to become adults that you will be proud of.

In September of this year, a Scout-a-Thon was held to raise money to send deserving scouts to the 14th World Jamboree in Norway. The cost of this month long trip is approximately $1000 per boy which includes a number of optional post Jamboree tours with details to come in the near future.

It was unfortunate that the goal was not reached in this event but the Trenton District Council has voted and decided to send eight scouts to Norway, one way or another. Cases are known where boys have been denied the opportunity to attend one of these Jamborees due to lack of money. Are we going to tell these eight boys that they can't go because we have not got enough funds to send them? Maybe you would like the job of telling them – I don't.

I am telling you not to deprive YOUR scouts from Trenton that opportunity and experience of a lifetime. On behalf of all the members of the Boy Scouts of Canada and of the boys from my town and yours to help raise the necessary money to send these boys. The initial registration fee of $100.00 per boy must be paid by December 15th which has already been taken care of by the Trenton District Council but your help is needed financially.

Don't let these boys down. Remember when you were a lad and what would you think if you were told that there was no money to send you so you would just have to forget about it. The boys that have been selected as representatives of Trenton are all well qualified and have been carefully screened by their leaders and members of the Trenton District staff.

Contributions to "Operation Nordjamb 75" will be tax deductible and will be placed into a special account with our objective being at least $6000 to be raised by May of 1975.

How much can you or your organization give? Contact me if you have a donation?

Yours in Scouting,
Cecil Paul, Public Relations Officer,
Trenton District Council, Boy Scouts of Canada.

NOTE: People of Trenton must have read my plea for donations because the eight boys went to the Jamboree in Norway. According to a letter to the editor of the local newspaper on June 29, 1974, money was being raised to send two deserving scouts to Norway.

I never voted to send eight boys when we were so desperate for funds at that time.

Not one scout of the eight that went to Norway ever came back to the District Council and thanked them for all their fund raising efforts.

Scout – Guide Week 74 Called Great Success
By
Cecil Paul, Public Relations Officer
Trenton District, Boy Scouts of Canada

Half a million strong is the slogan for Scout-Guide Week '74 and it was chosen because we believe that it's time for us to realize that we have tremendous number of the youth of Canada in our program. It is growing more and more each year and it would be even greater if we could get more adults into the scout movement.

The Trenton District Council put a great deal of time and effort into making this week long celebration one to remember for years to come.

The Trenton Sing Out Group entertained for the Movement on Wednesday night at the High School. By the sound of the applause, it was a great success.

The History of Scouting on Stamps, which was prepared by Cecil Paul, was shown to the group after the singing and it gave a history of Lord Baden Powell and how scouting has spread to over 150 countries since its beginning in 1908.

If the weather permits, the week will get a good wrap up in the form on a Cub fun day which will be held at Frankford Game Club on Saturday afternoon starting at 1.30 pm.

The District skating party will be held on Tuesday night at the AMDU skating rink starting at 7.30 pm and will be open to all members of the scout and cub groups in Trenton.

Dear Mr. Cornish,
Editor, Trentonian.

On the suggestion of one of the members of the District Service Team, I sent a copy to Lady Baden-Powell in England for her scrap book.

Last week I was very pleased to receive a letter from Lady Baden-Powell herself. You must remember that she is 84 years old on February 22nd of this year. It was very gracious of her to take the time to write this letter as I am sure she must have a tremendous amount of correspondence to answer.

I would be very much appreciated if you would print a copy of this letter to your readers as I know there is a message in it for all of us – whether we are involved in scouting and guiding or not.

Thank You,
Cecil Paul, Public Relations Officer
Trenton District Council, Boy Scouts of Canada.

Hampton Court Palace,
East Molesey,
Surry.

Dear Mr. Paul:

I have just received your nice letter and with it the cuttings from your newspaper telling the story about your Scout-Guide Week, and including quite a lot of valuable information about the movement itself.

I hope all the celebrations of your special "Week" went off well and successfully, and that they will have a helpful effect on the stability and the development of the movement locally.

We are growing in quality and in quantity all the time now, and there is no doubt with all the sad things happening in the world today, people are turning to Scouting as being something really good and worthwhile in the lives of the on-coming generation of young people, and more adults are volunteering to become leaders.

I hope that this may be the case of your Trenton District, and that all your groups are in good heart.

With thanks for your kindly letter and best wishes to you and all your members in all positions in Troops and Packs, and may happy success come to them in all their tasks.

Yours very sincerely,
Olave Baden-Powell,
World Chief Guide,
Vice President Boy Scout World Association.

BOY SCOUT PROGRAM EXPANDS – The Boy Scouts of Canada added a new official program to their organization last month. The Beavers, boys from the ages of five to seven years old, were officially made a part of the Boy Scouts of Canada on November 15, 1975. This experimental program has been running for two years with the first colony being formed in Winnipeg, Manitoba.

The Beavers came to Trenton on September 18th with the 10th Trenton Beavers being formed and sponsored by the Kiwanis Club of Trenton. They meet every Wednesday night at Marmora Street School. 30 boys registered in Trenton to form the 10th Trenton Beavers. A long waiting list is on hand and in the near future, a new colony, as they are called, will be opening at Dufferin Street School to accommodate these boys.

They have had two meetings so far, with the boys having a great time. It seems the leaders are getting just as much out of this program as the little guys. Vickie Paul, better known as *Rainbow*, is the senior leader at Marmora Street, and she has a load of assistants. The boys are divided into lodges of six boys each with their own leader. Jack Jesty is the male member of the group which is a must. He is a man with experience, having worked with Beavers before coming to Trenton. The group at Dufferin Street will be known as the 11th Trenton Beavers.

In 1978 my close friend in Scouting, who was also my brother-in-law Ken MacKay, was transferred to Peterborough, Ontario. He was a member of the Canadian Armed Forces and it was time for him to leave the Trenton area. Clarence Whitman had also retired as District Commissioner.

I decided that I had enough of scouting and I also retired.

I believe that I had accomplished a lot in my years with the Trenton District Scouting program. I made a lot of lasting friends through scouting. My two sons had lost interest as well so it was time to move on to another venture. If it is as rewarding as my time in scouting, it will be well worthwhile.

Donation given to Cablethon

Among the donations presented to Cablethon '78 Monday night for Crippled Children was a cheque for $368 from Cecil Paul of Trenton. Mr. Paul is shown talking to the host of the Cablethon Norman Post, left. Mr Paul presented the cheque to Ian Darling, right, standing, who represented the Trenton Rotary Club.

The money was raised from pledges Cecil got for racing his wheelchair against the clock at 708 Communications Squadron, which will be explained in a separate article.

I spent 12 years writing newspaper articles for the Brighton Speedway which took care of my Saturday nights from May until September. Besides the local papers, I wrote a weekly column for a Toronto based newspaper called "*Wheelspin*". I also wrote a weekly racing program, kept track of the races and their order of finish. My articles, at times tended to make some people unhappy but I wrote them as I saw them. Race fans vented their displeasure in the *'Letters to the Editor'* on a regular basis.

RACING FOR A GOOD CAUSE

Benefit race for the handicapped
A five-dollar bet that paid $657

With a look of satisfaction, Cecil Paul grabs hold of the tape signifying he has completed his one and a half mile wheelchair race in less than 20 minutes. His efforts produced $657 in pledges for local handicapped adults and children in the Trenton area.

It all began in November, 1976. Cpl Harvey Kirby, a teletype operator, and co-worker of Cecil's, ran his compulsory one and a half mile run in 8 minutes and 53 seconds. Captain Kent Craig, the Commanding Officer of 708 Communications Squadron, presented Harvey with a certificate of his record-breaking achievement.

It was at that time that Cecil Paul, a civilian communicator and long time employee of the Squadron, said that he could do a mile and a half in 20 minutes in his wheelchair. The Deputy Commanding Officer, Captain Reg Brinston, who happened to overhear Cecil make his bragging statement, bet him $5.00 he couldn't do it.

Cecil decided that if he was going to do this, why not make up sponsor sheets with the money going to a good cause.

Officials from the Base mapped out the course, which followed a route around the parade square, down to the recreation centre and back up behind the Base Hospital to the parade square. Despite the intermittent rain, dozens of supporters crowded the finish line at the CFB Trenton parade square as Cecil Paul piloted his wheelchair across the tape.

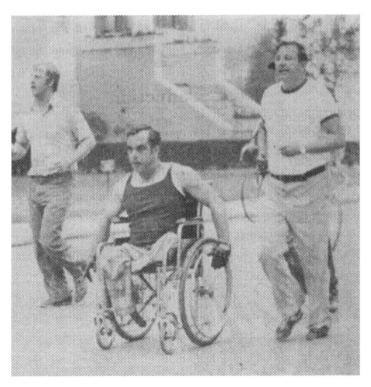

Cecil Paul rolls along in his wheelchair, making good in his race against the clock. Two friends paced him as he made his run.

He did the course with time to spare.
His time was 18 minutes and 56 seconds.

During a social gathering and celebration after the race, Captain Kent Craig, 708 Communications Squadron Commanding Officer bet Cecil $5.00 that he couldn't do it again next year – faster than 18:56 and the challenge was accepted.

Cecil Paul aims for a new mark. He is hoping to do the measured course of one and a half miles in less than 18 minutes and 56 seconds. This is the time he ran the course a year ago.

The race will be run on the same course as last year and it is hoped the weather will be kinder than it was in 1977 when it drizzled most of the day. Pledge sheets were made up again in 1978 with totals expected to reach over $1500.00, with the money again going to the handicapped adults and children of the Trenton area.

Saturday, June 24th, 1978 was the date set for the re-match with Sunday as a rain date. This event was now known as *Operation Hot Wheels*. On a warm sunny day, Cecil made his second run for the money. The second race was over the same course as the initial race held a year ago. He collected another $5.00 bet, this time from Captain Craig as he crossed the line in 17 minutes and 14 seconds. It was one minute and 14 seconds faster than his first time. The good Captain wanted to bet Cecil that he couldn't do it again in 1979, faster than the 1978 time. Cecil declined and figured it out and did the math. He would be another year older, besides he had proven his point by winning the original bet two years in a row.

Ian Darling, representing the crippled children's fund and a member of the Trenton Rotary Club accepts a cheque from Cecil Paul, a long time employee of 708 Communications Squadron. This took place after Cecil had collected pledges for winning a bet two years in a row.

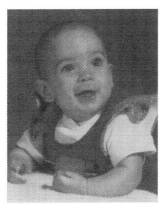

**Our family got a little bigger when Vickie
gave birth to a bouncing baby girl.
Jaime Elizabeth.
She arrived on November 6th, 1976.**

The Magnificent Seven

History was made in 1976 when seven original members of 708 Communications Squadron were all back again on transfer to *Thumper Squadron*. The *Magnificent Seven* were all here in 1964, when the Squadron was originally formed. 12 years later, they all returned for at least their second tour of duty and some for the third time. One exception was Cecil Paul, the civilian Communications Operator in the front row. He never left. In fact, he is still with the Squadron. He plans to remain until 1989 for the 25th Anniversary celebrations. It will be the year that he completes 35 years of service at Canadian Forces Base Trenton.

Front row, left to right: Jim Wall, Cecil Paul and Norm Williams. Back row, left to right: Roger Moses, Norm Pickle, *Skip* Anderson and Neil Burke.

Working at 708 Communications Squadron was not all work and no play. During the winter months curling was the big sport with bonspiels held at least once a month and I decided to give it a try.

The hot rum toddies sure warmed me up and made the cold a little more bearable.

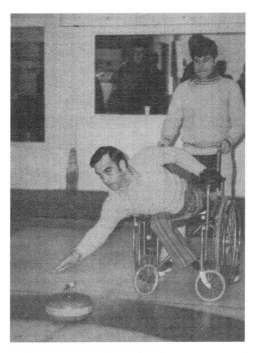

It was not that difficult. I was allowed to have someone hold the back of the wheelchair so it wouldn't slide on the ice. I was no Glen Howard but I was part of the gang and nothing was ever mentioned about my chair. My acceptance, to me was another case of everyone treating me like one of the group. That was very important to me.

One morning my son Steve and I were sitting having a coffee when he suggested we start a softball team and enter it in the *Greater Belleville Softball Association.*

We did some checking around and there was room for a new team. All we needed was to get a sponsor and find some good ball players. We approached Tim Hortons and they agreed to sponsor us. They would buy the uniforms and pay the other necessary expenses connected with a new team.

We attended the spring meeting of the Association and picked up some players. Steve managed to find some more guys who wanted to play on a new team. By opening day, we were ready to play with me as the coach.

Greater Belleville Softball Association "A" Division Champions

Front row, left to right: Gord Nicholls, Cecil Paul, coach, Scott Maracle and Mike Butler.

Back row, left to right: Chris Denike, Darrell Lott, Sean Deline, Chris Hewlett, Russell Plummer, Steve Paul and Greg Nolan

Not bad for a first year team in the Association.

In 1979, I reached a milestone at CFB Trenton - 25 years continuous service in The Public Service of Canada.

Cecil Paul is being presented with a plaque commemorating 25 service in the Public Service of Canada. Doing the honours is Captain David Heath, Commanding Officer of 708 Commsqn.

It is said that this was one of only six such plaques signed by Prime Minister Joe Clark due to his short term in that position.

Cecil Paul, a Civilian Communications Operator employed at 708 Communications Squadron being presented with the Commander's Commendation and Commander's Citation from L/Col D. Ross, Commander of 70 Communications Group Trenton in August 1984.

Communication Command

Commandement des communications

Citation
Commander's Commendation

MISTER C.S. PAUL
708 COMMUNICATION SQUADRON, TRENTON

FOR OUTSTANDING CONTRIBUTIONS TO THE MILITARY AND TO THE COMMUNITY AT LARGE

Mister Paul has been employed within the military community since 1954 and has, since then, consistently strived for excellence at his place of employment and in his outside activities. In addition to his primary duties he has demonstrated a willingness to get involved in various projects and organizations that have benefited the military and the civilian communities. His involvement has resulted in the writing of the "History of Communications" complete with a large map presently proudly displayed at 708 Communication Squadron Headquarters. He published a book "A Guide to the Grading of Canadian Coins" which has been widely distributed, he worked for a local speedway newspaper, he was the public relations officer for the Trenton Boy Scouts as well as the District Cub Master. He was assistant editor of the Canadian Forces Base Trenton Newspaper "Contact" for a year. He organized wheel chair runs raising money for the crippled children in the Trenton area through the Rotary Club of Trenton. He has himself, at times, been a keen participant in wheel chair races. Mister Paul, for his selfless contributions to the community and his untiring efforts, is a most worthy recipient of the Commander's Commendation.

**This is a copy of the citation that I received from
The Commander, Communications Command in August 1984.**

708 Communications Squadron Commanding Officers
Past and Present

Along with six of the previous Commanding Officers of 708 Communications Squadron over the past 23 years, Colonel CG Diamond, CFB Trenton Base Commander, attended the 6th Annual All Ranks Mess Dinner as a special guest.

Front row, left to right: CWO AC Hillier, Squadron Chief Warrant Officer, Major GJ Monaghan, Commander, 70 Communications Group, Group Captain CG Diamond, Base Commander, Capt DR Hounslow, current Commanding Officer, 708 Communications Squadron, CWO WG Fallows, Group Chief Warrant Officer and Mr. Cecil Paul, employed as a Civilian Communicator 4, for over 30 years. He has worked with all of these Commanding Officers plus four that are absent.

Back row left to right: MWO LR Willits, 70 CommGrp, Maj. (retd) WR McKinnon (1964-1967), Capt. WA Karau (1983-1986), Capt.(retd) JO Hicks (1972-1974), Capt. (retd) WW Laasko, (1969-1976), Capt. JP McDonald, (1974-1976) and Maj. (retd) WC Jackson, (1967-1969).

In 1984 everything was going good – I had a great job and my family life seemed great. It was at that time when Vickie's and my age difference started to have an adverse effect on our relationship. She asked for a divorce which I agreed to. She moved out taking our daughter Jaime with her. It was not long after that she remarried – this time to a guy in the military. A year later, they were transferred to Wainwright, Alberta. Jaime would come and stay with me during the summer holidays.

My son Steve was working as a waiter at a restaurant in the Quinte Mall in Belleville called *Tudor Arms*. He and one of his co-workers decided to play cupid. It seemed Denise, his fellow worker and he was working on getting me a date with her Mother. She lived in Toronto and came to Belleville every weekend where she stayed at her Mother's place. It would be easy for us to meet because I spend most of my weekends at *Tudor Arms*. I could usually be found at the bar, lubricating my system with rye and coke. Denise's Mother was a buxom blonde called Gloria. She was divorced and was single at the time. We were introduced and the rest is history. That was in 1986 and we have been together ever since.

We went to Florida with Gloria's brother and his wife that year and had a fabulous time. It was not long before Gloria quit her job in the big city and came to Belleville and moved in with me.

Gloria has two children – a boy and a girl and I have my family consisting of my oldest daughter Lynn and two boys, Steve and Wayne and a younger daughter Jaime.

Wayne also worked at the restaurant, but in the kitchen as a cook. Everyone got along great and they still do.

Gloria and I in 1986

It took three times but I finally got it right. It hasn't been perfect because we have had our differences over the years. We have learned to talk things out and we have had a great relationship which has lasted over 30 years.

After I retired in 1989, we travelled extensively to various destinations which I will tell you about later on.

Lieutenant Colonel AR Brown, 70 Communications Group Commander presents Cecil Paul, a civilian Communicator 4, with his silver medal after he completed 35 years in the Public Service of Canada. Major DR Hounslow, 708 Communications Squadron, standing in the background, smiles his approval.

In 2009 Gloria and I decided it was time we got married. We

figured a courtship lasting 23 years was long enough. We hoped that we should know each other by now.

A quiet wedding was planned with our families only. I don't know what happened but 76 people showed up. The ceremony was nice with a great reception afterward.

Gloria and I on our wedding day

"MAN IN MOTION" COMES TO TRENTON
– 31 October 1986 –

The *"Man in Motion"* tour arrived at Canadian Forces Base Trenton, where a large crowd was on hand to welcome Rick Hansen as he continued to wheel across Canada, on the last leg of his round the world wheelchair trip. This was not only a historical event for the Base but for 708 Commsqn as well.

Colonel CG Diamond, the Base Commander was unable to be there so he asked Cecil Paul, a long time member of 708 Commsqn, who is also confined to a wheelchair, if he would present a cheque, on behalf of all the Base personnel to Rick. Cecil said that it would be an honour and a privilege.

To Cecil! Best Wishes!
Rick Hage

Rick Hansen accepts a cheque for $2600.00, from the personnel of CFB Trenton. The official presentation was made by Cecil Paul, a long time member of 708 Commsqn, on behalf of the Base Commander.

Cecil, like all other Canadians, had been following Rick's progress since he left Vancouver BC. This was an excellent opportunity to meet the man who had become a National hero, not only in Canada, but throughout the world.

25 YEARS LATER
– 31 October, 2011 –

Once again, Rick Hansen came back to the local area - 25 years to the day when he came to CFB Trenton in 1986.

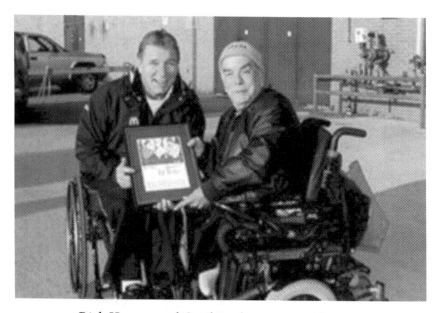

Rick Hansen and Cecil Paul renewing old times.

Cecil is showing Rick the picture that was taken 25 years ago.

It was autographed by Rick when Cecil presented him with a cheque from the personnel of Canadian Forces Base Trenton.

The original picture was a Polaroid snapshot, taken on October 31, 1986, with Rick signing it on the white space at the bottom of the picture.

Cecil spent close to half an hour visiting with the *"Man in Motion"*. The amazing part of this return visit is that Rick remembered Cecil and their visit at CFB Trenton.

This was one of the highlights of Cecil Paul's career. He can't make up his mind which time was the most memorable – the original time in 1986 or the reunion 25 years later.

We purchased our mobile home in the Sunshine State with my severance pay. We spent a lot of winter months there in the sunny south.

Most of our families managed to come down for a visit during the cold weather. It was not a cheap place to own as we had to pay lot rent year round even when it was sitting vacant during the summer time. When the Canadian dollar fell to 75 cents on the dollar, we decided to sell it at a big loss. We just couldn't afford it any longer. We have many fond memories of our times spent there and the many friends we made.

Cecil Paul and some of his published books
City philatelist puts stamp on book publishing career

Belleville's Cecil Paul wants to put a Canadian stamp on Philately. Philately is more commonly known as stamp collecting and Paul has written a book to be published in March 1992, which chronicles Canada's history in Commemoratives stamps.

Entitled *"From Sea to Sea"*, is the culmination of six years work by the 56 year old Sidney Street man.

"It started with a stamp show in Toronto. A friend of his thought his display was worthy of a book. What started out as 66 pages is now 146 pages. He's hoping the book won't just inform Canadian readers, but also open the eyes of our neighbours south of the border, where stamp collecting continues to flourish.

Writing is nothing new to Cecil. This will be his third book, in addition to hundreds of articles for magazines, newspapers and journals. His first book, A Guide to the Grading of Canadian Coins, was the first of its kind when it was published in 1964. He also wrote a 25 year history of 708 Communications Squadron at CFB Trenton.

The writer hopes his history in commemorative stamps will meet with the same acceptance as his first effort, the Grading of Canadian coins.

His book on coins sold 6,000 copies in it first month in 1984. That was at a dollar each when dollars were harder to come by.

In 1986, Paul turned to stamp collecting seriously and decided he would focus on commemorative stamps.

"Definitive stamps are the ones you use to mail letters with. Commemorative stamps are issued in smaller quantities and celebrate an event, a moment in history or a person."

"A stamp collector just puts stamps in a book. A philatelist learns the history of a stamp and the purpose for its issue"

Paul's book will feature Canadian commemorative stamps from Canadian native people and Inuits to the first Canadian in space. Readers will not only see the stamps but also get some history on their subject and the reason for being issued. The book will include every Prime Minister who has been honoured with a stamp.

"Living people cannot be honoured with a stamp unless they are a member of the Royal family or the Governor General. That's why when Canada issued its space stamp, you didn't find Marc Garneau's face on it."

Paul is the only Canadian columnist with "*Stamp Collector*", an American monthly paper based in Oregon, on the hobby.

Cecil's book will be published by Paris Graphics of Paris, Ontario and will be available at Leisure World outlets across Canada.

Switching to Coin Collecting

Local Numismatist
Writes Book on Coins

Cecil Paul, 3 Ramsay St., a well known numismatist in Trenton, winner of several awards for coins and coin displays, was the guest speaker at the annual North York Coin Club in Toronto.

Mr. Paul spoke on the grading of Canadian coins. The grading of coins is a very controversial subject, said Mr. Paul, and a specific standard is needed. He went on to explain the ways to judge a coin for wear, pit marks, scratches and mutilations.

A book on the grading of Canadian coins has recently been written by Cecil Paul with the assistance of Gerald Parker of Philadelphia, New York.

The book with illustrations drawn by Mr. Paul, deals with only the wear caused by normal circulation. It explains the various conditions of coins in the categories of uncirculated, extremely fine, very fine, fine and very good.

Soap Box Derby Racing

In 2000, my son Steve, his six year old daughter Heather and his eight year step-son Travis were looking for something that they would all be interested in. They all agreed to try soap box derby racing.

The first race Heather competed in was at the Frankford Soap Box Derby. She was the only girl in the derby – winning the title of *King of the Hill*. Steven took the two kids and competed in several different derbies in the area for the next couple of years. Their travels took them back to Frankford a year after Heather won her initial race and she won the main event again.

After winning this event three years in a row, Heather suggested they rename it and call it *Queen of the Hill*. The officials said they couldn't do that. Steve decided to join the *Canadian Soap Box Racing*

Association. The CSBRA held races from May until September in venues throughout the Province of Ontario with their main track being at Kawartha Downs in Peterborough, Ontario.

Steve asked me if I would like to join them as they were going to a CSBRA sanctioned race in Smith's Falls one Sunday. I was happy to be doing something instead of just sitting around all day, so I agreed to go.

From that day on we never missed a CSBRA sanctioned race over the next four years. We also attended two non-sanctioned events; one in Windsor and the other in Gatineau, Quebec. The race event in Quebec was very interesting and educational as none of us spoke French but we managed.

The Association didn't have a web site so I volunteered to design one which I maintained for those four years complete with photos of all the winners and posting up-to-date information, plus keeping track of their racing point system.

Heather loved the sport especially when she was beating the boys every week.

Heather and Travis raced in two different classes. They would never have to race against each other that way. Heather raced in the Masters Class and Travis ran in the Super Stock class.

Steve and I came up with the name the *Pinkinator*. Heather and her car were unbeatable three years in a row. She loved racing and had fun beating the boys. She was the only girl in her class.

In 2006, Heather outgrew her car. You would understand if you knew how she had to get in her racer.

Steve designed a car just for Heather. Where the Pinkinator was downright pretty, her new car was the ugliest thing on four wheels. It started out as *Masters Class* racer and ended up as a *Hobby Pro Class* car.

He cut the top off the car so Heather could drive sitting up rather than lying down as she had to done in the Pinkinator. He then cut several inches off the nose to make it the required length for a *Hobby Pro Class* car. It wasn't much to look at but it was very aerodynamic and was undefeated in 2006.

In the same year I received the *Director's Award* from the Greater Peterborough Soap Box Derby Association.

With Travis and Heather both leaving the sport, Steve and I closed the book on four years of great fun and fond memories.

Life was getting boring after we sold our mobile home in Florida. Gloria was doing home care for some little ones which led me to spend a lot of time alone – too much actually.

I was up at the Quinte Mall one day when I was approached by an old friend who asked me if I wanted a job. Mark Hanley owned eight Tim Hortons franchises in Belleville and he asked me if I would like to come and work for him. I had coached his softball team a few years back and he has always called me *'Coach'*. I worked evenings for the next four years as a drive thru order taker at one of his outlets and I must say, I got pretty good at it and was a familiar voice on the five to 11 shift. I then worked two more years at the Hanley Corporation head office where I was in charge of the surveillance cameras which were located in all eight locations. These cameras were in place to watch the employees and keep them honest. You would not believe the different ways these so called *'loyal and honest workers'* were stealing from the company.

I was not very popular with some of the employees but it was not a popularity contest. It was a job that I became very good at and Mark was also happy with my work. I think I made a difference over those two years – cutting crime by a large margin. People were hesitant about stealing when they knew someone was watching them on a full time basis.

In 2005, we decided to take a cruise so we booked a Caribbean cruise with Carnival Cruise Lines. We had to fly to San Juan, Puerto Rico where we boarded the ship called the *Destiny*. Carnival said their ships were the fun ships and they were right. We had a fabulous time.

Don't we look like a couple of real cool tourists?

The following year we went on another Carnival cruise aboard the ship named *Liberty*. This time we sailed out of Fort Lauderdale Florida.

My wheelchair is my legs. I have to depend on having a wheelchair that is comfortable, solidly built and with a small wheelbase. It has to be comfortable because when I get up in the morning I am in my chair until I go to bed at night. I have never sat on my chesterfield or in a chair other than my wheelchair. It has to be built for the outdoors as my chair is my only means of transportation. I love getting out and about as much as possible, weather permitting. I ride my chair to the Quinte Mall and the Bayview Plaza. They are both about 3 miles from my home.

I am entitled to a new chair every five years. A Provincial Government program called *Assisted Devices Program (ADP)* pays for 75 percent with me paying the balance.

The last chair that I purchased through ADP was a piece of garbage. It was less than two years old when one of the motors blew. The warranty had expired and the cost of a new motor was over $800. It was more money than I could afford. I applied to ADP and was told that I would have to wait for three more years before I would be eligible for a new chair.

A friend of mine had a small wheelchair that he would sell me for $350.00. It was not fancy looking but looked like a good buy. It was small and compact which I had to have. My chair has to have a narrow wheelbase to get through the doors in my apartment and this chair fit the bill. It was great to get my independence back which is very important to me.

February 13th, 2012 was a bright, clear sunny day and I decided to catch the bus and go up to the Bayview Plaza. I planned on stopping at Kelly's Home Health Care to say hello to my son Steve who works there.

I was crossing the intersection at the Loyalist Plaza entrance near Captain George's Fish and Chips, heading for the bus stop. I never made it. A vehicle travelling north on Bridge Street West swung into the intersection and hit me broad-side. The impact knocked me and my chair about eight feet with me hitting hard onto the pavement. As I wear a seat belt all the time, the chair landed on top of me. Two guys who were standing on the sidewalk came to my rescue. They helped me up and got me back into my chair. The driver of the car claimed he never saw me and he seemed very upset. He immediately called the police while I sat and tried to gather my composure. I'm not used to flying through the air and crashing onto the pavement with a wheelchair on my back.

A policeman arrived and wanted to know what happened. We both explained the incident to him. He wanted to know if I needed an ambulance. I was still in shock and told him that I was okay and I told him that I didn't know how much damage my wheelchair had suffered.

I got a wheelchair taxi to go to Kelly's Home Care where my son was working. When I arrived there, my son Steve said that I was acting strange and was quite worried about me.

Steve checked my chair over and said the frame was bent and it had several cracks on the side that was hit. It was still driveable but very hard to steer.

I went home and decided to lay down. After a couple of hours, I began to have pains in my left arm. My wife insisted that I go to the hospital to be checked over. My arm was x-rayed and I was told I had a cracked bone in my elbow and was given a sling for my arm, the one I use to control my chair. A further exam of my elbow a few days later showed it was not broken, just badly bruised.

The next step was to contact the owner of the car that hit me and explain what had happened. He didn't seem very concerned and told me that he would have to wait until he could read the accident report from his insurance company.

I battled with the owner of the car for almost a year. He refused to buy me a new chair and told me to get a used one. I explained to him that wheelchairs are custom made for the individual and I had to have a new one built for my specifications.

It was time to get serious and I got a lawyer. He told me they could sue the car owner but it would take years to settle. I needed a new chair now so he decided to get in touch with my home insurance company. He contacted them and they agreed to buy me a new chair. I was told that it would not affect my rates in any way. In less than a week I received a cheque from them for the full amount of a new chair.

My new chair was top of the line and the cost was $9962.62. My insurance company told me they were suing the driver that hit me. They said they would get the full amount for the chair back from them. I received my new chair exactly one year to the day after the accident.

Brighton Speedway Wall of Fame inductees for the year 2014, were, left to right: Paul Turner, driver, Cecil Paul, Public Relations Director and Peter Bontius, also a driver.

I returned to Brighton Speedway on August 2nd, 2014. It had been 40 years since I was last there where I worked as Public Relations Officer. I was invited back with my family for a very special occasion. The Speedway has a '*Wall of Fame*' with three new people being inducted each year.

For ten years I spent my Saturday nights during the racing season keeping track of the point system for the drivers, scoring the races, doing a racing program plus writing a weekly column for the Trenton and Belleville newspapers as well as a column in the Toronto racing paper called *Wheelspin*. During that ten year period, I never missed a race. I even got married on a Thursday so as to not miss a racing event.

It was a very special night as my family and myself got to sit up in the booth along with the race announcer who was a long time friend of mine - Huck Flindall. I was the man who gave Huck his racing name for all the years he ran in the six cylinder class. Everyone knew the *Flying School Teacher* and his familiar number 57. Huck Flindall made the presentation to me that night when my name was added to the wall.

I look forward to my daily early morning coffee with my son Steven. We meet every morning for our cup of java from Tim Hortons. You might say we're regulars when you don't have to tell them what we want. They usually have it ready when they see my wheelchair coming across the parking lot.

Steven is not only my son – he's my best friend.

My son Steve and I relaxing over our morning coffee.

There you have the story of my life. It was not all good or all bad. I have had my moments. I don't have a bucket list like some people. I have had what I consider, a very full life. I have seen a lot in 80 plus years. I am very proud of my accomplishments. They have not been earth shattering but I am satisfied.

I have a fantastic wife and a great family who support me 100% in everything I do. I have tried to live a normal life, whatever normal is. I may have a few regrets but I believe everyone has. I have never let my handicap stand in my way and have never had time to feel sorry for myself. I have always tried to keep busy, with no time for sympathy.

The things I am thankful for are my friends, my family, motorized wheelchairs, accessible city buses and Tim Hortons on the corner.

Finally, I have always believed that *walking is highly overrated*.

Printed in the United States
By Bookmasters